INVITATION TO VIEW

Peter Scupham was born in Liverpool in 1933. His childhood was punctuated by Lancasters, flying bombs, National Service and Cambridge. He has shared a working letterpress with John Mole, lectured, taught and has, with his wife Margaret, rescued a 400-year-old house and garden. His *Collected Poems* (Oxford/Carcanet) came out in 2002, followed by *Borrowed Landscapes*.

Invitation to View
Peter Scupham

CARCANET POETRY

First published in Great Britain in 2022 by
Carcanet
Alliance House, 30 Cross Street
Manchester, M2 7AQ
www.carcanet.co.uk

A CIP catalogue record for this book is
available from the British Library.

ISBN 978 1 80017 210 4

Book design by Andrew Latimer
Printed in Great Britain by SRP Ltd, Exeter, Devon

The publisher acknowledges financial
assistance from Arts Council England.

CONTENTS

For Margaret, who has kept my poems and me alive, also for Chris, Kate, Roger and their Mother.

With huge gratitude to Michael Schmidt, who has supported me wisely and wittily from PNR *1.*

WHEN

When you close your eyes,
lamplight, sunlight,
there they all are —
a host of invitations:

birds at frosted crumbs,
a terrier's pirouette,
enough blue sky
to patch Dutch trousers.

Catch as catch can:
the pitch of their voices
hurries off the words
to the grand silence.

Her hair is shot silk;
his jacket hangs just so,
the bricks of their playhouse
tingle with love and shadow,

hiding the question:
'Where shall we go,
when, for the last time,
you close your eyes?'

NATURE

His eyes calm, level:
'I had a dream last night
I know now there is no such thing
as the subconscious.'

From under his bed
crept this creature,
darkening the space
between floor and door.

Its voice knew the crunch
of broken biscuits:
'I am Nature
I have come to get you'.

There he stood,
suit pressed, tie straight,
cheeks glowing pinkly
from a close shave.

I watch those eyes
fix, then cloud.
On his cluttered shelves
the books play kiss,

Locke on Education
walking out in leather
with a paperback doll:
'Zazie dans le Métro'.

Under the bed
stuff chaws and mumbles,
nests between the lines
of tomorrow's obituary.

STICKING IT OUT

For Anthony Thwaite

They're sticking it out today: sages, poets…
There's Doctor Spooner with his stalking wick,
a host of Marsh-land Georgians with blackthorns

and Mr. Thwaite, his ferrule twisting molehills,
hoping the velvet gentleman has paddled him
a Samian fragment or a clipped denarius,

his feet robust, well-grounded, even at times iambic,
and with Ben Jonson, his 'learned sock' well on,
taking new illumination from old footlights.

We brandish our armaments, or leguments —
my prop for Aged Hippies, Morris-flowered,
dating from the dagger in my femur —

and set our quarter-staffs at sharp riposte
while Charon watches from his pleasure-boat,
murmuring the name he chose for his dark water.

DR GAUSS

Just off the Winterstrasse, I think.
Appropriate: dogs leashed and muzzled,
black coats and female furs,

snowflakes drowning in your hair
and a sky that promised little
but more of itself, and that the same.

No reason to climb the stair at all,
Dr Gauss. Kuriositäten. We sensed
things tinkling, wary of wet sleeves

or less appropriate domiciles.
Locked. A door closed softly.
I think I saw him from the window,

neat, hair *en brosse*, bespectacled,
scurrying towards the Marienkirche,
nursing two ill-shaped packages,

but you, laughing, said you'd seen him —
lanky, blond, dangling a bird-cage —
swing left into the Zoologischer Garten.

No matter. But whose desk should it rest on,
that stumpy chunk of bone we found,
lipped over a rattling musket-ball

when we unpacked our foolish trophies?
And that card, in long-dead Fraktur,
Fröhliche Weihnachten!

WINTER WORDS

Calendar pages:
one scrumpled day
dies in a garden

spun to fool's gold,
where wind mews
over twigs and bones

at an outhouse door,
black sky sustains
the buoyancy of loss,

dried sap
knots branch to branch,
caging a star

whose variable glance
is light's tumult
cut to the quick

yet cold to the retina
as once upon a time,
remembered pain.

OUT OF REACH

Think of a hand-slip,
a spun summit
bothered by mist,

the whirr and thrum
of dark metals,
a stranded face

minding a gap
which widens, widens,
leaves one candle

to burn in silence,
late summer wings
to char on glass,

unspoken words
to spell their spells
forwards, backwards —

fine fruit to hang
in armouries of thorn
for the devil to spit on.

FOR GOD, KING AND COUNTRY

Flags and flowers:
three bloody years
worked in silk.

At the needle's eye
stand easy, ghost,
slip through my fingers

your blue, indelible,
weightless kisses
for the children.

Tell Charlie, Min,
time is short now.
Up to the firing line

for night operations —
a 'fabrication française'
where threads unravel,

unvarnished truths
must be embroidered
by cheery cards.

Not the only one
not by a long way,
your loving brother

Albert.

MYNHEER WAUWERMANS

From the long ride, fresh trees
licked by enough blue light
to cross-patch antique trousers,

we come at last past casks
head-dressed with tulips
to this puzzling concourse

where white signs agree to open
a house decked by strangers
with an attentive love.

'Mynheer, do you remember?
Yes, twenty-five years.'
Our polls are whiter than old snow

but your children are fresh as paint,
rocking softly to a lullaby
sung by a Dutch doll in a carved bed.

Shall we make solemn playtime,
hiding our wiser faces
in crimson velvets, rusty tassels?

Over there, in the English pub —
the Wagon and Horses —
a soft tom-tom thicks the air

to a stuffed smell in a dark pocket,
the press of occupation,
smoke rising.

GOODMAN'S GARDEN

Where did they all go?
Thickets of love and pain
rustle in a dry light
and skeins of corvidae
traipse to a dusk roost.

Time is a flip book.
Lift your dear hand
and feel the pages purr
as years fan by
in their lost variegations

of green, gold, brown,
and an old cat,
white as a child's Christmas,
trots a careful way
through his once kingdom.

THE CUTTING EDGE
12th December, 1935

That day,
they opened the Pavvy at Bexhill-on-Sea.
Chermayeff and Mendelsohn dreamed it to be
a people's palazzo, a go-with-the-flow:
a mural by Wadsworth, the chairs by Aalto,
an aesthetic of now: glass, plywood and shiny
steel ribbons, clean concrete, the purr of the briny.
Such bold cantilevers and covered-in walks
greeted 'Buck' De La Warr and the still-uncrowned Yorks,
such a tucket of fanfares, of plaques and tall-talks.
        Posh tot on a chair, with my nicely-brushed hair,
        gaiters and gloves and some buttons to spare,
        I was lurking in camera, but very elsewhere,
            little me.

That day,
with its high-booted morals buffed up to a shine,
the Lebensborn eingetragener Verein
was founded by Himmler, Reichsführer (SS),
for his black-hearted blonds in their fancy-pants dress —
most unlike their four-eyed and pasty-faced boss
with his Totenkopf stare and his cartwheeling cross —
to be fountains of life, scatter-braining their seed
on the purest of Aryan Mädchen, who'd breed
pretty Kinder to warble the Horst-Wessel-Lied.
        On that studio chair, in my soft woollen coat
        with its natty back-belt, buttoned up to the throat,
        my gaze locks on yours, playing rabbit and stoat,
            little me.

LEONIE'S GARDEN

Dishevelled, whispering,
leaves are telling us
how this cultivated ground
welcomes each small trespasser:
fieldfare, moth and ladybird;

offers a liberal education
in Latinate taxonomy,
the construction of nest and web.
Graduals of light
build swaying towers

of crimson, gold and tawny,
find their echo
in cool rooms whose fabrics
wear the smoky brilliance
of a tarnished rainbow.

Moored lightly to the wind,
her flowering boat
will drift us through the seasons.
Fruit ripen to image:
labour, to contemplation.

ADVENT

Yes, they say, how the days draw in,
how all our summers gutter down
until the light can hardly lift itself
to find life crouching in its nest of fur,
the late fruit shrivelled, the charred wick
twisting away from the ghost of flame.

Darker still, where a dead house
puts bricks of broken cloud together,
and children you can no longer name
share loneliness with twigs and birds,
the dry abrasions of a missing gate
awkwardly swung between then and now.

Step into the night beyond the kitchen door,
let rooms decked with heat and laughter
greet the cold, astonished air,
as your breath feathers you out and further
than those bleak reaches hope must traverse
under the disposition of a star.

Pity you didn't know us in our day —
We might have found you sitting by the lime
in sleepy summer, or in scented May
at lunch with Peter looking for a rhyme
he'd kicked into the long grass by the pond
and Margaret tickling some old cat. Yes, fond

of desultory stuff as life went by
with frogs and flowers and idiotic talk
under trees shuffling green about the sky.
We're sorry that you couldn't break your walk,
unlatch the gate and find the front door wide
on chequered shade and bric-a-brac, inside

find rooms life found itself too short to dust
and cobwebs that went back an age or two,
spot a Ravilious plate and Shakespeare's bust —
old brochures say just what old brochures do:
'A house of books and pictures'. Cakes and tea?
A pleasant might-have-been — but let it be.

We'll watch you puzzling at us from the lawn
until the faces hidden by our names
turn into whispers, rustles, all forlorn
as maidens, crumpled cows and played-out games.
Don't tell us who you are — we needn't know.
The dark will tell you when it's time to go.

THREE NIGHT SONGS

For Anthony Thwaite

1: Standing here

Standing here, where the skyline falters
into thickenings of the dark, as cold
presses itself against itself, a wrap
snagged on a bramble patch of stars,

you could look for love, like a boy
adrift in a lost lane, waiting it out
through a maze of years, a puzzle of faces,
for light to spring from a hidden window.

Looking for love, you could stand here
holding hands with the dead, the night wind
hovering lightly as a wayward kiss
in the quick brilliance of an unshrouded moon.

2: A little further

Asleep in the lodges of the night,
you sense them by the absence of your senses:
the old dog, stiff in his Sunday coat,
the letter never sent, nor even hoped for.

A little further — that nest of shine and splinter
where the first kiss meets the last on a cold forehead —
you need a music, lost outside the cradle,
to sound these depths, unlace this intricacy,

tell them what they once tried so hard to tell you.
The night beds down among its tears and moss,
makes no further preface to revelation.
A choral silence gathers, intense and helpless.

3: Listen to the voices

Listen to the voices that ride the air,
shaking Orion in his long stride:
the broken morse of drifting owls,
the growl of wind in clung leaves;

find yourself lost for words
which might decode these messages
where trees, hunched over glimmerings,
tell small tales of pain and hunger.

Tremble when the dead brush by you,
weave a spell over your cold hands;
glimpse a passing tongue-tied angel,
wings feathered by a secret love.

WALKING THE WALK
For John Nolan, Orthopaedic Surgeon

It's ball and socket stuff:
crawl on the kitchen floor
then 'Look, he's standing!'

Under starter's orders
trudge the pavements,
swing, dodge, scamper,

do starfish drill,
hunt for shrapnel,
pound a barrack square,

put a best foot forward,
for the long march home
up hill, down dale;

brown thins to grey,
grey blows to white
in the keening wind,

but taken to pieces,
braced and bolted
like old Meccano,

I'll walk on eggshells,
walk the walk
and talk the talk.

Let's go.

SUMMER 1954
Remembering Ray Kinross

Let Saint-Malo put its golden self together
where you came a purler on the tramlines,
ravaged France crawl towards and past us.
Windily we head-butt wounded ghosts
down gritty avenues of dust and poplar,
swung valleys, cluttered by old stone:

Tinténiac, Chinon, Langeais, Saint Mars,
Rigny-Ussé, Angers, Orléans…
In a rowdy bar in a particular nowhere
Michelle's blonde hair teases to smoke,
as she waves back into our futures,
becomes kisses on a Carte Postale.

Montsoreau's fishermen can only see
long wands tapering out of time,
floats hovering on crushed silver.
I watch you yawn, feel for a Caporal;
our propped bikes mesh their shadows
to a lean tangle of dark and bright-work

while sun savages our noonday dawdle.
Come on, tighten toe-clips, a quick swig
then, crouched over dropped handlebars,
rough-ride the pavé, bounce and skirr
past staring children, gossip mothers,
your beret jaunty, my jerkin open.

Let name shake into image, image blur,
air loosen its hold on long-lost luggage.
Scout for an auberge, Ray. I'll catch you up —
just half-a-sec to ease this chafe and ache:
head down, unstrapped, and hurt by bright
on the dust road I can see nothing, nothing.

TAKE YOUR BOW
For David Horovitch at 70

Hats, periwigs or firearms say
someone, it seems, has gone away,
and who are those left standing where
applause hangs scribbled on the air?
A black bag props a tilted chair;
house lights bring up the day.

Was it a ghost, that go-between,
who slipped us on from scene to scene,
who stitched the living to the dead
who turned the fire in someone's head
to flesh and blood, a dance that said
more than cold words could mean?

Off, off you lendings, and for now
back to your cupboard love. Allow
the boards to be but floorboards, all
the fear-struck room, the painted hall,
to find out moonlight, wait their call —
Come, David! Take your bow.

CAT ICE

Wake on a blue morning,
find a sky you could fall through,
greet your childhood

and those long slides
from the shouting playground
into a happiness

whose slivers break
from the crazed surface
as you do your cat-dance

over eastern tinklings
while the cold
deepens, deepens,

and the night tells you
how thick ice offers
as much as you can bear.

CYCLIST

His voice eager,
the timbre light,
he adds words daily,

defining hillocks,
twists of water,
the lane's corner

where a flung bike,
dazzled in the sun,
scurries into silence

as a vanished summer
conjures it all
to a slow dissolve

and what he is
leans from a window
swung on a far garden,

glances, puzzled,
at a brilliant shadow
leaping off the grass.

A SIX SPOT BURNET

Sprawled out beside this roadside pole
and nothing in the air but the same
and same again, the lightest trill
inside his crooked arm, inside the pole,
inside the air which stays, will stay the same,

a blue softening to ache, a dream
strung on, between, over the wired sky
whose high, sweet songlines mesh
through a boy's head caught in a June dream,
which flicks away from the song, the sky

to the road's verge, grass high and dry
where a Six Spot Burnet sways
and sways again, a shiver, tremble
stirring the crinkled wings which dry
bright metals, as the boy's head sways

to the milky ache, the dazzle of light,
the tarred verge, trill and shiver, the song
as moths unsheathe summer from its pale cocoon,
stumble and purr away into the light
into the swaying head, the ache, into the song.

CINNABARS

Rust, moths, moths and rust
daggers of wicked glass,
sloughed off seat-skin,

the Model T crouches
in a sea of ragwort:
'Yak-ya, yak-ya'

sing village children
as I swing the wheel,
heel and toe

the frozen pedals,
clock back summers
till aunts and uncles,

the builder's children —
Jack and Tommy,
Midge, Doss and Billy —

jump from their graves,
dancing, flying
clean through me

and cinnabar larvae
in stripy jerseys
munch out our salad days.

EN PLEIN AIR

A page stares back at the sun's brilliance;
a pen flickers, tugs: a kite's tail
winding a simple message into the blue.
Words tremble in a fluster of ribbons

where a host of small particulars
hovers between visible, invisible:
spume, spindrift from a swollen sea
dragging its rhythms there and back again.

Under a wind iced by clouded water,
the richest lexicon dwindles
to the kiss and sting of sand-grains,
as, long ago, a bleached face,

jounced over metalled thunders,
stared from a carriage window
where a pother of smoke and smut
ground lost words into ancient light.

CORONATION

One Christmas morning
I heard myself sing
to a steaming kitchen
'I'm as happy as a king

belie-eve-mee',
things going to pot
and everyone doing
the turkey trot.

As happy as Henry
and his court of beeves,
basting his fat
for My Lady Greensleeves,

as the snow-starred baby
in his candled stall,
they say is King
and Lord of all,

as George the Sixth
and his cigarette,
coughing over Margaret
and Lilibet,

whose words will struggle
to be great and good
through Marconi's
fretted wood,

while twists of tissue
go stammering down
uneasy heads
that bear the crown.

builds itself out of deepest dark.
Under a pelt of thatch and frost
chamfered bone shivers in the wind,
shivers in the eastern wind.

We shrink into otherness; our fingers whiten.
The house is our nest of apprehension,
a cavern of ash and sighs where rats tap-dance

as Daisy, Dapple, patched out of moonlight,
strike flown sparks from tumbled cobbles,
whinny in the break and tangle of our dream.

We had not known the inside was so out,
the droves of night so full of watching,
the out so in, swung doors at sentry-go

as the dead with owl-faces and bleak eyes
busy with milk-pails, whips and ribbons
cross sill and threshold in a dry-leaf hush.

The cold, such cold
where cats creep out of their garden-graves
to keen in the wind,
to keen in the eastern wind.

MONSIEUR CLERMONT

That August, in la France profonde,
the frelons were out in force,
honey-gold cruisers of the late summer air,

their poignards sheathed. The heat
lapped at our sticky terrace table,
an observation post for village fictions —

Jean, his bench-saw snoring to the hornets,
a girl scraping her pans out for the hens,
that old man in his garden chair —

le petit vieux. We smiled as if our smiles
could throw a tremulous lifeline
to one who seemed to have no need of saving,

a kindly ghost, a dream of summer silence,
the gentle answer to our drift… of questions.
That last day, when Jean came for the keys —

'Nos amitiés à votre père, monsieur' —
he tapped his forehead, murmured 'Verdun',
carried our cases to the little Peugeot.

Yes, I remember growling hills,
flickers of white and violet light —
cartwheeling bayonets trophied to the dark,

the way our farewell smiles, careful, elaborate,
glanced off that casemate of a skull
where Monsieur Claremont had been taken prisoner.

RIDERS TO THE SEA

For Sydney Harrod

Swan Vestas: a scrumpled coffin
surfaces in a forgotten drawer:
'Stones from Yeats's Grave'.

The curtains time has gathered
ease a little for the Irish light
to dance its watery veils for us

free-wheeling now, after sixty years,
still riding westward, stowed gear
weighing no more than a handful of dust

old money light in our pockets,
showered with gifts and amazements:
colour-washed houses floating by

our bent heads filled with poems,
a girl, a grey house, the fuchsia's blood-gouts,
dreams unpunctured, bones unbroken;

our flaming meths skitters into the night
from a tent pitched on a stony hill;
an old woman keens to her spinning wheel.

Galway, Connemara, Sligo —
'In Drumcliffe churchyard Yeats is laid' —
bending down in awkward reverence

I steal chippings from the grey shroud
hiding that suspicious jigsaw
packed off home from Roquebrune.

Two cold-eyed cyclists passing by
on the long way home, one with a matchbox:
'Stones from my grave'.

Deep, deep, in the dark wood,
past the gingerbread houses of the poor
in their tilted hats and jittery bones,
he came across a pediment of shells,
their nacre daisy-studded on the night.
The leaves that overhung were stains of muslin,
historic with misery as a widow's sighs
in her dowdy parlour. She stood at the portico,
as she had stood for centuries, her glad-rags
teased out to scraps of nothing by the years
that crawled with broken backs across her feet:
little Bo-Peep, alone in the Vaults of Death,
the simulacrum of a lamb nuzzling the twigs
that passed for fingers. Such tufted wool,
caught on the barbed-wire of the past,
such bleating, such innocence and slaughter,
while, in the clearing where the bomber fell
in its flurry of smoke and pain, he counted
on the scorched earth, seven scorched trees
but did not know their names...

THE POKER-WORK OWL: 1944

Cows moan in grey: a broken lullaby
from soft throats grazing on the early stars;
the big Merlins growl in Lincolnshire
where a boy arranges his shadow squadrons.
Hunched in an icy cockpit, he rides
to join the thunders drawling overhead.
Night-scented stock eases up its pallor,
a prying moon makes ape-face in his mirror.

He swings out of bed, pads to the stairhead:
black, contrapuntal voices. A door slams,
its thrill shaking the house as a freight-train
rearranges the frontiers of the night
in jostles of buffered metal. Pinned to his wall,
a poker-work owl sees nothing, says less.
Shrouded cotton curdles into absence;
his curtains cross themselves for luck.

MRS WRIGHT'S BUNGALOW

For Jane Griffiths

Pulled out of dream, the hush, hush water
longed for, trembling, out, out beyond
the smoky spire of the fat candle,
a room losing itself beyond its edges,
the hush, dark but gentle, the trembling,

feet padding, bare toes, the shaking,
the candle clutching its yellow flame,
murmurs, wrappings, holding of hands,

the room vanishing into cloud, the storm
quivering the prom, the boil and crush
of water rummaging, the grips tightening,
the child's eyes widening into salt white sea:
childhood calling, drowning, going down.

EPITHALAMION

An acrostic for Sam and Laura

Summer and love: Sam, Laura, fur and feather
At nature's prompting lair and nest together;
Magic and logic in this case agree,
And yet, some say, two into one won't go,
Never a chilly flame or burning snow.
Don't two hearts mingled end up one? We see
Logic in love has crooked ways to run —
A starlit daytime meets a midnight sun.
Under time's wings the landscape slips away
Racing its flowers and cities into clay
And magic's logic conjures 'I' to 'We'.

MARTINSELL

I was a dancing fiction of that night,
a shadow stretched from shadow, where the trees
grew into stars prickled among leaves
twitched out of memory and goblin-town.
I followed branch and stem, placed cool hands
on each cool vanishing, but could not move
beyond the crooked ring they broke, re-joined.

Tonight, I wander the dark floor of things,
count the sawn trunks of years that lie
felled in front of the grim hedge of sleep,
follow the light bobbing above kept secrets —
my guiding star, my ignis fatuus —
and ask once more what company I kept
that midnight hour in once upon a time.

THE ENCHANTED PLACES
For John Fuller

Were you there
when the moonlight split in two to let the bombers through,
the angled iron gun-dogs began to growl and bark
from the leashes in the park,
that fury, that crescendo, that despair
tearing gobbets from the sky just as they'd been trained to do
while night slid down the chimney pots to thicken up the dark?
Were you there
when the street took so much rain there was water on its brain
and a stranger put his arm round your imaginary friend?
Did you know it was the end?
Parcel, string and sealing wax — but nothing there to share.
Could they kiss away the solitudes of pain
when you spun your paper boats away to lands of let's pretend?

Were you there
when from the rock-pool sand they brought you back to land?
The sun scorched on the sky had other fish to fry
and though dead you could not die.
When they sent a dreadful message to the kite-tails in blue air,
did worm-casts coil about the beach in hosts of ampersand?
Did anybody, everybody, think they had to cry?
Were you there
when the house of ought and must, of anxiety and dust,
tried to loose a tongue-tied love — but a raven-hearted dove
who knew push must come to shove,
pecked the words out, and picked the letters bare?
While the cold moths in the box-room went to rust
did the kittens in the bucket share that love ?

Yes, I was there,
glitter-dazzled by the places where shellfire left its traces,
and the coloured scrunch of living that crawled across the floor.
Now the heart grows raw,
grey tides crinkle, things falter on the stair
I wave to other children with their cold and missing faces
my fingers feeling for their light through myriads of war.

STRANGE MEETING

Jouncing along, in an old wooden carriage,
I looked in vain for some lost dream-girl
needing protection from a desperate marriage:

five fellow-travellers. Formal, pale and stiff
I looked at their unlooking from the corner
left for my settling, and considered if —

that saturnine young man in battledress,
hair slickly shining from its centre parting,
his Sam Browne dancing to the light's impress

could be — was really — Wilfred Owen. He
looked idly out, where wires looped and swung,
and stationary cows rushed by. But not at me.

I nudged my case, and stared. In it I knew
was the unwritten poem I had made
knitting the done to what was left to do

until the Sambre canal ran into epitaph.
Writing his name in sour and sluggish water;
I could have asked him for his autograph —

not quite my style. Here is the poem, though,
that lay in waiting, and which cannot ease
those miles and hours the past must undergo.

LUX IN TENEBRIS

I

That Christmas bauble —
a crimson blood-gout
tined with silver —
pierces to the heart.

And Richmond china?
Fred and Dorcas, the 'young roe',
have scraped their plates bare;
they'll need no washing.

This light sees through
their conversations;
small talk drifts
from another country

whose tongues I learned
at mother's knee.
Under the tree tucks
one late parcel.

Whose head stamps it —
paper, string, sealing-wax —
the knots too tight
for these old fingers.

II

But the tree shivers,
silting down
its pins and needles.
In huge cold

a procession moves
down Himmelstrasse
to the savage pits,
the broken cross.

Cut the string,
unwrap the paper;
there is nothing there
for latching fingers,

only darkness,
folds of darkness
clouding the lawns
of a tarnished playtime:

the sigh of earth
gone back to earth;
forgotten runes
that bring no healing.

III

The house throws light
from its Jack O'Lantern,
horse-bones dry
in deep foundations.

Is the witch-bottle set
under the hearthstone:
scarlet wools,
pin-pricks, urine?

Salt-glazed bricks
cling to the chimney;
a poker crosses
two black grate-bars,

and circles, stars,
cupped horseshoes,
let sidling whatevers
go back to watching

Yule logs char,
deep sleep deepens,
cats bring mice
for propitiation.

SEASONAL

For Margaret

I

Now, stretching itself after a sleep
this animal thing shrugs its greening pelt.
Tethered stuff nods and sways itself about;
a thousand eyes break open

and all those implements of garden surgery
flash their serrations to the coming light.
The garden meets your strictures, hand in glove;
small lives hop-dance

as it turns itself over, flexes its claws.
Hold life up to the light, see clean through it,
each droplet curled on a pulsing spectrum —
limb, petal, thorax.

II

The concourse halts, sun-struck. Girls and flowers
change their dresses. The garden draws its breath
and all its decked inconsequence runs for shade.
We watch time standing still

as if we know (much virtue in 'as if'),
colour must riot while it can, not play sober-sides,
shaking its cloths about like a mad haberdasher
caught in wonderland.

Then that familiar, strange Chekhovian sound,
the distant gong that heralds the main feature,
the laughter flung down in the face of time,
the heart adrift, and breaking.

III

Sack-cloth and ashes. Put it all to bed,
let everyone share our passion for dead leaves
twirling in their equinoctial circles,
gazing up from ancient faces

as we move in our heavy coats to festivals
where the past barrows its urgent ghosts
to purifications of memory and flame,
eyes gather the silt of dreams.

We hang by a thread from the vanishing light,
as the diadem spider depends on its nest of dew,
the cratered apple hangs over its fall,
the sword from Orion's belt.

IV

Behind cloud-scraps, between the branches,
stars wester. In this cold harbour
the delicate savagery of last summer
stiffens into shadow.

Tonight you can lift your eyes to where,
steepling from far to far, the light years
ride to earth down filaments of zero,
taking their time, our time,

to patch the garden with forgotten voices,
disclose a country of dead shells and whispers.
Listen. The frost aches, the bright imago
sleeps in its dark chrysalis.

HOUSE WORK

For Norman and Chris

Now we must cage our lives in a palace of air
raised up as a child ladders a box of bricks
or slides the playing cards into a tower —
kings and queens perch on their flickering thrones
by a space for cooking smells, the kitchen cat

you might glimpse now, scaffolded on high
waving his tail to the most invisible stars.
When the rag-a-bone house shakes off its lendings,
Norman and Chris will take the whole thing's measure,
consider the greenwood, and the tigerish light

which eddies and flows about them as they space-walk,
dancing a wall-plate over the spalled bricks
rehearsing their daily story of two on a tower,
carrying loads of sunlight back into rooms
where vanished children play with a dancing cat

and the palace of air swings round them, and about,
as playful as Escher, severe as Mondrian.
They are our saltimbanques, our smiling acrobats,
easing the weight of the world as that kitchen child
eased a coloured straw from his haystack cluster,

as they balance the house on a sigh, a swirl of air,
and a patchy sun strokes down the fur of the bricks.
Night will stare down at their absence from its tower,
thatch with velvet the echoes, the roofless rooms —
the crooked house arches its bony back like a cat.

PAINT AND PAPER

For Mark Hearld

Give us a room. A rug, some chairs will do,
a bed, a table — crooked walls, rough-skinned,
a window-square for watching day and night
watch us work out their shifts, play me and you;
beyond, robin-song twists to owl-call, wind.

Time now to load the brush, unpack the heart
and hands. Find us blue eggs, a freckled thrush,
or better, two, to sing their doubled song,
a dumb-cluck cock to strut the door, then start
on birds in hand worth two in any bush:

a painted dove to ride our mimic sky,
to lift our talk, to preen the kitchen air,
and stolen from some backyard slats and wire
a clutch of nid-nod hens to prowl and pry
for grubs and grain unscattered on the stair.

Your gallant creatures catch the morning light
their cadmium yellows and cerulean blue
sparkling their furs and feathers into life,
as Yeats's painted horses roamed the night,
but trembled into stillness, wet with dew,

at dawn. Let your diorama bring them all:
a snow-lit house to gather wild and tame,
each footfall soft, their kingdom peaceable,
born out of love and coming as you call,
each freed and held by its own proper name.

THE COLD SPOT

For Christopher Reid

'There's a cold spot here, Terry?'
'You're right, John. It's a cold spot.'

That's it, you see. The astral visitor
sucks heat in hope to turn it into substance,
as ancient gentlemen stood, backs to the fire,
treating their bottoms while the ladies froze.

Our two plasterers were adepts both
at covering up old manifestations,
laying, layering them with hawk and float,
each the other's doppelgänger.

'There's a cold spot here, Terry?'
'You're right, John. It's a cold spot.'

One tall, one short, but names handy-dandy.
Which was Terry, which John? The years
are adept at diminishings. On lucky days
we can just glimpse a working hand,

or movement in the air suggesting one.
Doors and windows corner our half-glances;
those are the places things home in on.
Listen. Is that a message from The Beyond?

'There's a cold spot here, Terry?'
'You're right, John. It's a cold spot.'

Lime plaster: spectral in its nature
soft and sticky, white and malleable.
Hard now to read their faces, catch their eyes,
possible, just, to catch those Norfolk voices

alert for old-time murder on the bridge
at Acle, growing warmer, colder,
moving slowly about our rooms in hiding,
stretching the letter 'o' to double zero.

'There's a coold spot here, Terry?'
'That you John?' 'Terry... Terry...?'

Man playing cards with his dog,
up in the lost attic. Found dead.

Playing dead? No. Real dead,
stone cold. The Ace of Spades.

Cards on the table. Happy families
beggar their neighbours. Snap!

With attic salt flavour your tall stories:
Watch Shuck, fiery-eyed, black dog.

Man's hunchback bends for dog to ride on;
shadows lurch by candle-light.

Dog must have done it: Snap, Snap;
how the cards fall faster, faster.

CHIMNEY SHOE

Shoe, shoe, little dirty-feet.
Who are you, to scurry through walls,
slip through an ache of centuries

and leave a shoe tucked in the chimney
for our imagination
to paint you as the light chooses?

Take yourself off to fetch and carry,
diddle diddle dumpling, my son John,
one shoe off and one shoe on.

A witch mistook the shoe for you,
crept inside, mumbled on nothing;
did you feel her pins and needles?

Backwards, forwards, one-step, two-step,
plates to scrape, floors to scrub,
we feel the quick wind of your passing

through long-gone spick-and-span, voices
calling you back from a pinch of dust.
Shoe, shoe, little dirty-feet.

THIS DARK SEASON

Dusk unwraps our familiar otherness:
a swung gate, a tip-tap at the window,
an old cat rummaging for sleep
in a greenhouse, that frail hutch of gleam.

Step out, pause where the tree-line anchors
a floating pasture of cloud-shreds:
a deer, a fold of moonstruck shade
waits as custodian of that silence

we knew when, adrift in our lost gardens,
we, too, moved as the air moved, lightly
picked up by time, dropped as dead leaves
pluck from their corner to lie down again.

In this dark season of gifts and strangers,
we balance the moment: rough grass
and star-peep. Eyes trap the solitude;
old bricks drowse and tremble in the cold,

your hand in mine goes whispering
as a wand of light conjures night adrift
over a presence step-changed into absence.
Stiff branches ease back into conversation.

GARDEN SHAKESPEARE

I

Trees push up high
for an upstart crow.

Narrow a sharp eye,
they look like scenery,

those trunks bold, undulant:
a wooden O

to make less pliant
this love-locked greenery.

Take the old house away,
its bricks, lit panes

too full of yesterday.
Untangle a space

for laugh, shriek, sigh,
dancing in chains

where words trip by
but know their place.

II

Under tree scaffolding,
over beaten bounds,
autumn rides on summer.
Words flick shine

from now to ever now,
leaf to leaf: words
thrown against all
that travels towards us

in dark and wind.
They hold their audience
to its loss and loving,
as those dust faces

drifted in back years
caught and held them
before sky language
made words birdsong.

Spores and seeds,
a dressed lexicon
to people the stage
of our wayward garden.

'WHY, THIS IS SESTINA, LADY!'

Shakespeare in the Garden —
For Kevin and Linda Crossley-Holland

Are they then real, as real as this sestina,
the painted faces and the painted sky,
the pretty dolls unwinding skeins of words?
We are the gardeners with our nets and hands
to catch the syllables before they fall
and falter in the grass, until they die

to rise again, because we know to die
is consummation, union a sestina
perfects unless the schema rides to fall.
We've touched the roses up and scoured the sky,
juggled the sulking seasons. At our hands,
nature and Art are both subsumed in words,

or, as the Prince would have it 'words, words, words',
before his tragedy said 'Time to die',
in darkest consummation. Uncross those hands,
applaud the entrance of the fair Sestina
whose grace and gravity weds earth to sky,
whose strains and swains shall have no dying fall

unless her melancholia suits the fall
of all those touched-up leaves, autumnal words
that lend our comedies a lowering sky.
The tree-house rocks, the breezes rise and die,
tied canvas swells and bellies this sestina;
actors and audience play on, their hands

adrift on laps, or holding other hands.
Dancers weave by, counts mourn and rustics fall
to puzzling jest. Sestina? Who's Sestina?
Enter a cat, stage-left, real fur, no words,
it knew no more that it was time to die,
that dead mouse trophied up against the sky,

than these, our dear semblables. Evening sky
crawls on to resurrection. By clapped hands
puppets and puppet-masters live or die
but which is which? The starlit curtains fall;
we are the prisoners of ghosts made words,
their glad-rags coffined up in a sestina

where masks and masquers die to live, blue sky
brightens Sestina's landscapes and our hands
let nothing fall; nothing is lost for words.

A DOOR

And, if you open a door,
what you have placed there comes to light
as the sky moves in from the window
to pause, notice the chest of drawers,
a cat's pricked ears,
your carpet's teased-out fringes.

But can you discover words
for the frisson, the trip-wires hung
from fear to love, both lost but hungry
to ghost you scents, a tune, a place
where the carpet
lies flecked with foam, the sand's rim

runs out to the sunburnt grass;
a tartan rug, a biscuit-tin
flicker and vanish. The chest shadows
a girl whose face is patched with tears;
her gingham frock
blows to curtain in the wind,

the cat, in its garage box,
stiffens in its long sleep. Whose hand
gathers yours, as you cross to the bed,
shake yourself awake, but dreaming
of tumblers, matchsticks,
and, if you open a door...

THE SHIMMERING CAT

For Bertie, the Snow-Spotted Bengal

Legs far too long to reach the ground —
so, stepping high, he walks on air;
sand, cinnamon and rumpled lace
weave the coat this cat must wear,

whose dapples shift like water-rings
bounced from the path by summer rain,
or clouds which sail their sunlit cusps
down drying puddles. Dyed in grain,

that shimmering camouflage must hide
the secret cat beneath the skin,
mortality transfigured there:
an angel dancing on a pin.

With flick-flack tail and haunted stare,
with eager ears and lime-white throat,
he sings of life in the greening year,
the cat that wears the Joseph coat.

THE KIOSK

It shone in its coat of silver,
its name lived under and over
in a tremble of magical whispers.
The news looked black in the papers,
as black they said, as your hat.

Railed round, bushed up, it sang
with a sad and wavering song,
there were no doors, no eyes,
no love for that desolate voice,
no one told me what it was at

as it glimmered away in the dusk
full of questions I dared not ask,
hunching the squat of its shape
to perch on the ledges of sleep.
It lived there, and that was that.

There were things going on and off
and the nights were full of stuff,
but there in the darkness of risk
it sat and sang: the kiosk, kiosk,
with the cloudy purr of a cat.

CATCH

I caught it for a moment
as it slipped the raindrops;
between two notes of birdsong
it moved from light to shade
faster than old eyes could corner it.

Sand grew hot between the toes.
You called 'Butterfingers',
Mocking, yet minatory.
Who you were the east wind knows.
I stumble on these vanishings

as one stumbles on a bird-bone
in dark woodland, a petal
in the mortuary of a dry book.
All I once held, I hold
dancing between stretched fingers

where love and longing play
in slow tumbles of dust,
the drifted lexicons of loss —
a catch-as-catch-can
of words: homeless, flying blind.

REFLECTION

Looking at blue, looking through blue,
he watched slow floaters rise and die;
flowers were talkative that high summer,
their fluid crimsons bedded on his retina
as he twisted sunlight from his eyes,

took a steady breath to ease the skin
soaped on a clay pipe bowl, watched
a perfect globe imprison his reflection:
his charmed soul, perfect in its wandering,

to float it all away: the trill of voices
the dog's gruff coat, the cradled branches,
and all that curvature of space and time
which held him briefy, as life holds him,
carried through iridescence to his vanishing.

INDIAN SUMMER

A drugged sun
works in the cat's fur,
needling the tips to gold;
each stubble-stalk
is flèche d'or, sun-shot.

In a green stockade
wooden faces
make long shadows,
each feathered head-dress
just on the turn.

Stones and tokens
drag at short days
which ache to leave them,
to float dark skins
on a couch of stars.

Slipping light's noose,
two buff doves
in stiff jerkins
nod us through
to a colder season.

FOR ANNE STEVENSON

1933–2020
Lament for a Maker

Dear Anne, our shooting star, you've left us all
'*your lovelies weeping on a far away shore*':
husbands, friends, loves, admirers — a host
who suffered your hilarious devastations
tense with quaking joy. I see your hands
compassionately poised above my birthday cake,
the steel plied deftly. Though it winced
the blood was swiftly staunched, and we were left
with crumbs of sharp, sustaining comfort.

Oh, attic nights, when salt could lose no savour
rubbed in the wounds your rapier-talk inflicted.
As hours grew smaller, your imprecations
and efficacious 'fucks' rose up the chimney
to make Orion blush, or Father Christmas,
as poets known, unknown, yet to be born,
crept skinned and howling into dusty corners,
bobbed and hovered in the whisky fumes,
drowned in tides of laughter, fulmination.

Tutoring found you in a sprawl of drafts,
a chatter of poems flattering themselves,
loved to distraction by fond parenting,
while you, the musical philosopher,
rational magician, saw clean through them
as they read each other in woeful admiration.
Nagaina, cobra, how you fixed your prey
with unrelenting eyes, until that moment
when fear and folly turned to fun and feasting.

And now it seems that you have packed your bag
for one more residency in that country
you never could believe in, where Mr Darwin
at work on the fossil records of the angels
considers the embryonic state of wings,
watched by an affable chowder of young cats.
I glimpsed you as you hitched a passing broomstick,
your elfin face stern, yet benevolent.
Even white witches have to ride on something.

THE HEART OF THINGS

Slowly, the old house has pulled the night
about its bones, and wears it like a shawl.
Tonight, we sit here deeply by a fire
which warms the stretch of all those hands
the house wore down to skin and bone,

its flames the pulse beneath these coverlets
of paint and plaster; they talk of life
in that soft whisper and collapsing glow
which tells us how the dark and light are one,
in a soft bandaging of tears and laughter,

and lamplight rippling at the window pane,
watches time hovering about the room
in streak and bauble, scrats of winter weather.
And look, the cat sings to its ghost, ears cocked,
eyes bright from seeing into the heart of things.

SEARCHLIGHTS

Once, he pushed the garden gate aside,
found a cold, rough field, where quiet shapes
built a wonder-cage, a citadel of light
and whirling moths to scarify the dark

which crumbles away between his fingers.
Come, ghost-footed, over the grave of time,
old friends he never knew. Together
we'll watch the moon sink in a bruise of cloud,

and, trembling, a group of frosted children,
stare through the dust-motes of the stars
to where, beyond the blackest of black holes
angels dance, caught in their own radiance.

WALTER DE LA MARE: A LANDSCAPE

Always between, caught between wind and water,
hung between two notes of crooked birdsong,
the closing down of sun and the first star —
these are where you and your creations live,
spaces where, on the edge, darkness grows visible.

So, the return, threading again this landscape,
where a tall stranger on the muffled path
parries a courteous greeting with a question
his half-closed lips stammer to decipher,
wrapped in that solitude which is your own.

The connoisseur of secrets, he points you
to a gate swung open, a house whose welcome
catches your throat like first love's failure,
whose furniture is the rooms' guilty conscience
and the wrong sunlight shivers on the walls.

As children play the game of bones and shadows,
trapped by tall windows, lost in the riddle,
their knowing faces pale as dying candles
in air grown dusty-stiff as old brocade,
a girl presses her face against the glass,

watching a garden where bent age walks
between the scents of thyme and lavender
and a dead starling patches out the grass.
Whose memories shrivel in these neat parterres?
Time waits for a beginning, or an end,

but whispers you must leave to find yourself,
though finding yourself is what you came for.
Rooks wheel overhead in hoarse bravura:
that piece of paper on the garden path
the wind blows over — did it hold your name?

EVIDENCE
The Case of the Absent Signifiers

When the stripped house thrills to nothing more
than a rocking door, a wing-beat's flutter,
our tears and laughter long hung out to dry,
that deerstalker hat comes prowling the grass;
a magnifying glass sharpens meridian sun
as the evidence burns away in a curl of smoke,

just as a curl of wind in a far-off yesterday
loosed our smudged footprints off into the blue.
Tweedy, foursquare, the medical accomplice
gathers and notes for further prescription
a nail crooked in a wall, a dried mouse-skin,
a torn-off headline screaming of some disaster.

Insoluble. Traps have been set and packed.
Two missing persons have obstinately become
the shadows of lost knowledge: burnt diaries,
wardrobes, white goods, stolen kisses,
and all such herring-boxes without topses
as obstinately refuse light's blandishments

but prefer to increase the coverlets of the dark.
Will a new dig find 'fear in a handful of dust'?
Even Carter and his Mummy, bone-fossicking,
are gravelled for lack of matter. Glinting trowels
sift sandy soil; soil shifted, sifted, is soil still;
these burial chambers echo their puzzled voices.

Away, scholars, from our lost tumult of colour,
Where books read each other far into the night,
pictures grew windows for unretaining walls,
the garden sung the song-cycle of the seasons.
Let life play on with its grounded, green familiars:
a spring wind cut and shuffle our pack of secrets.

EVERY LINE IS GUARANTEED TO HAVE BEEN WRITTEN BY WILLIAM SHAKESPEARE

Sonnet 156

How heavy do I journey on the way,
For what care I who calls me well, or ill,
And threescore years would make the world away.
Make but my name thy love, and love that still.
Then, what could death do if thou should'st depart?
The earth can have but earth, which is his due.
When I am sometimes absent from thy heart,
O know, sweet love, I always write of you.
Your monument shall be my gentle verse,
My verse alone had all your gentle grace
For every vulgar paper to rehearse,
Dulling my lines, and doing me disgrace.
   When I (perhaps) compounded am with clay,
   The worst was this; my love was my decay.

Peter Scupham

EDMUND BLUNDEN: A VAGROM MAN (1966)

'You shall comprehend all vagrom men' — Dogberry

For Margi Blunden

'*Thank you for interrogation,*
A great help to a vagrom man' —
So, Edmund Blunden, his italic hand
holding the letters steady, things at bay.
though not beyond Dogberry's comprehension,
the two of them loitering at a green lane's end
by cottage thatch, an elmed rookery.

I forget the room: only the half-light,
the silence, the unsteady voice
tripped in twists between now and then
where his old England could not live or die,
wrapped in a ruckled sheet of meadow flowers
and sung to sleep by thrush and blackbird,
the fielders' voices calling from the deep.

'*I use ruled paper because it's all I have tonight*':
a vagrom man, to set the wits wandering
down lanes I half-remember, child of a later war,
where push-bike labourers headed into wind,
bent men drew their British Warms about them
and drugget wives gleaned hard harvests
from straight and cruel life-lines.

Helped carefully into the dusky rain,
he smiled with seeming shyness, and was gone,
ingenuous in his chosen artifice,
to search the dark for ghosts with mislaid names:
the *'harmless young shepherd in a soldier's coat'*,
whose flocks lay far and whitely penned
and would not rise to his long calling-home.
The Crowning (aka) Clowning Privilege.
Robert Graves, Cambridge,1954.

Too many walking-wounded. I was young
and green enough to have no care for them:
the Head, stuttering and blushing
over ribald Shakespeare, a thicket of nerves
crouched behind his bomber's plexiglass.
Closed looks, defensive anecdotes, quick angers:
now this barrack humour, mordant, undramatic,

delivered in the politest of clipped voices,
as we, last year's toy soldiers, man the benches
of Mill Lane's lecture-rooms. A craggy fusilier,
killed at High Wood, who died and rose again
to read his own obituary, opens rapid fire
on literature's old clothesmen and their dummies:
Such beautiful unfairness, cruel delectation

as targets rise in the butts, then, riddled, take their bow:
Yeats and his *'hard burnished rubbish'*, Pound
'sprawling, ignorant, indecent, unmelodious',
Eliot, visiting the grave of his poetic heart
with flowers, Auden's *'zinc-bright influence'*,
'sick, muddle-headed, sex-mad D.H. Lawrence',
the musical nonsense of Dylan Thomas —

These be your Gods, O Israel —
and not a fighting soldier in the lot of them!
Academe is a flutter of black dovecots
the word 'significance' is briefly court-martialled
and sentenced to death for congenital idiocy.
An ambushed emperor of the awkward squad,
he signs disdainfully my friend's 'I, Claudius'.

A BASKET CAT

A kitchen waits
for Christmas Day,
a basket cat
purrs time away

whatever stars
go wandering by
or portents cloud
the damaged sky —

sling-shot, gun-shot,
affairs of state,
a breaking heart,
a dropping plate.

Furred black as night
as white as snow
torched eyes to search
our ebb and flow,

in papery chains,
a scent of hay,
the basket cat
purrs time away.

C	Count your new tesserae for an old mosaic,	C
H	hang bauble, bird and star in their high hush,	H
R	ride dark and dream out for another year	R
I	Image, Imago, Magister, Magi —	I
S	shine softly, words, numinous as wet pebbles.	S
T	Traveller, caught where shadow greets the light,	T
M	mazed by this cold clench of stone, make firm	M
A	A Crib, a Cross. Let Lux Aeterna	A
S	seed your caught breath with a flock of candles	S
E	exhaling their halos over the quick and dead	D
V	Vale, Ave, Alpha, Omega.	A
E	Ease a studded door for your spell-bound entry.	Y

GIFTS

A stable. Add a starlit carapace:
A mimic theatre, one wall gone astray,
Open to such elements as compose our room.
The time? Oh, Quattrocento. Place? Let's say

Some beast-house near Firenze. Shepherd boys,
One necklaced by a lamb. He has no proper name,
Unlike those gaudy cardboard potentates
Still grimy from the ways by which they came

To spread their scents and lustres for a child,
Wawling in half-light, cornering his eyes
On Gyb the cat, slinking through stinking straw
To drop a dead mouse where the manger lies.